A PASSION FOR
Needlepoint

HAYAT PALUMBO

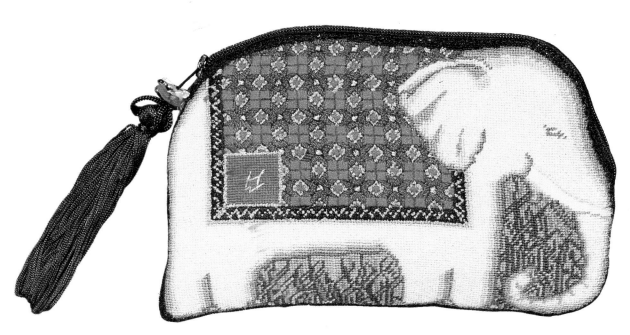

Photographs by Jean-Pierre Henfrey

NEW YORK

To Peter,
with whom everything
became possible

First published in the
United States of America in 1991 by
RIZZOLI INTERNATIONAL PUBLICATIONS, INC
300 Park Avenue South,
New York, NY 10010

Library of Congress Cataloging-in-Publication Data
Palumbo, Hayat
    A passion for needlepoint / Hayat Palumbo.
    p. cm.
    Includes index.ISBN 0I8478–1425–4
    1. Canvas embroidery.   I. Title.
  11778.C3P346 1991
    746.44'2 — dc20   91–512860
                                            CIP
Designed by Mavis Henley
House Editor: Suzannah Gough

Phototypeset by
Keyspools Limited, Golborne, Lancs
in Palatino
Color separations by
Newsele Litho Ltd
Printed in Italy by
Printers Srl Trento
Bound by LEGO Vicenza

Endpapers A counted-stitch design.
See page 156

PP. 2–3 A pair of Queen Anne cushions sewn
in *gros* and *petit points*

PP. 6–7 A seventeenth-century French
Louis XIII design

PP. 8–9 Detail from a French eighteenth-
century design. See page 58.

Acknowledgements

My grateful thanks go to all those at Weidenfeld and
Nicolson who have helped in making this book, and in
particular to: Michael Dover, my Publisher,
and Suzannah Gough, my Editor, for her smooth coordination
and patience; my thanks are also due to
Jean-Pierre Henfrey for his excellent photography,
to Mavis Henley for her imaginative designing
and to the stylist, Sandy Evans.

I should also like to thank Kerry Taylor who helped me
write some parts of the book, Prebendary Dr Chad Varah
for correcting my text and Cathy Chester for typing it,
and Lord Mishcon for his kind advice. Also Antonio and
Ana Bela Rodrigues for all their help.

My gratitude goes to Patricia, Lady Foley, and to
Susan Bates at Tapisserie for so competently and
efficiently gathering and returning to their owners
all the material photographed, and to
Mrs K. Van der Bijl in Paris for all those years
of friendly cooperation.

I am equally grateful to all those who agreed to be
photographed at home at such short notice.
I shall list them in order of appearance:
Mr Charles Smith-Bingham, The Duke of Marlborough,
Mrs Godfrey Bradman, Mrs Charles Hambro,
The Lady McAlpine of West Green, The Countess of Harewood,
Mrs Clovis William McAlpin photographed in the home of
her decorator Mr Christopher Rowley,
Mrs Gerald Ward,
The Hon. Mr and Mrs Steven Stanhope photographed on
the premises of George Spencer Designs,
Mrs Charles Riachy and Mrs Gilbert Jackson.

My thanks also go to all those who kindly lent us
needlework for photography. They are, in alphabetical order:
Mrs D. Anderson, Mrs E. Armaly, The Hon. Mrs J. Butler,
Mrs S. Burden, Mr M. Birley, Mrs M. Burrell,
Mrs A. Caldicott, Mrs M. Clark, Mrs G. Costa,
Mrs J. S. Cardwell, Mrs C. Chamberlain, Mrs A. Gresvig,
Mrs M. Gibson, Lady Hildyard, Miss L. Homfray,
Mrs D. Hart-Dyke, Mrs O. Harris, Mrs D. Kennedy,
Mrs V. Morgan, Mr C. McKay, Miss E. Mitchell,
The Lady Mishcon, Mrs W. Mond, Miss R. Michaels,
Lady Montgomery-Cuningham, Princess N. von Preussen,
The Hon. Miss A. Palumbo, The Hon. Mrs M. Parish,
Mrs D. Rosensweig, Mrs J. Streider, Ms N. Springer,
Mrs P. Spicer, The Marchioness of Tavistock,
Mrs W. Ward, The Hon. Mrs J. V. White
and Mrs C. Wemyss-Dunn.

And last but not least, my affectionate thanks go to
my husband and my children for their support and
understanding while I was busy with the book.

The photographer would also like to thank Kodak for
their generosity in providing film and
Metro Photographic (London) for their excellent processing.

CONTENTS

INTRODUCTION

Needlework has been written about extensively from historical, technical, and design perspectives. But to my knowledge, there has been nothing published which includes the people who actually practise it, except for historical personalities such as Mary Queen of Scots, Bess of Hardwick, Queen Victoria, Madame de Maintenon and even Louis xv. People writing in the past have lamented the lack of documentary evidence on the needleworkers themselves and I wanted to write a book about contemporaries from every walk of life, such as I meet every day in my shop, who continue to keep needlework alive and full of vitality. Although they do not constitute the main subject of this book, the eleven people photographed at home give a fairly good idea of the state of needlework at the end of the twentieth century.

For me, needlework has been a source of endless fascination and pleasure. I am moved by its hand-made nature and by the fact that it is painstaking even at its easiest. I owe it deep gratitude because it has been my refuge and my personal custom-made therapy every day of my life for a very long time. I learnt to embroider at school in Lebanon, and I immediately liked it; so much so that very soon, and for many years, my family and friends became inundated with my embroidery, which they were given as presents on every possible occasion. Little by little, I started expanding my horizons and, by trial and error, graduated from simple embroidery to counted cross stitch and from there to canvas work.

In 1986 I opened my shop. My idea was to develop a highly specialized and small business selling hand-painted canvases and the best possible materials in the field. Ignorance is sometimes a blessing because had I known what starting such a project meant, I would never have undertaken it. It was more of an adventure than a well-conceived commercial venture, but after two years the enterprise began to take off.

I was amazed by the spontaneous and generous response of all those we asked to lend us their needlework for this book just a few weeks before Christmas. Selecting from such a mine of wealth was very difficult but necessary with space limited to 160 pages. What touched me most though was the pride people showed in their achievement and the innumerable stories they told linked to their canvas work. For many, every piece of needlework is evocative of a particular moment in their life or of a person or an incident. But none is more poignant than Charles Smith-Bingham's story about his slippers. His mother, Jean, Lady Ashcombe, was killed in 1973 in an aeroplane accident in mid-air over eastern France. Her flight was put on a collision course with a charter plane by the French military authorities replacing the air controllers who were on strike; her aeroplane crashed while the charter plane landed safely with only slight damage. A few weeks after the accident, Charles received a telephone call from the airline informing him that a parcel containing some of his mother's belongings buried in the debris was on its way to him. When it arrived, there was just her bag of needlework with canvas and wool in it, intact. His mother had been embroidering for him a pair of slippers with an overall oak leaf pattern and his family initials 'SB' in the centre of each panel. She was halfway through the first one. Charles was unable to find out and will never know whether she was actually working on her canvas while on board or whether it fell 30,000 feet from her suitcase on impact. His wife Jennifer and her mother completed the slippers which he is wearing in this photograph and which have now become an integral and much loved part of Charles's wardrobe.

Hayat Palumbo

Slippers

Seldom do we come across a needlework pair of ladies' slippers nowadays. The pink bow with ribbons trailing lazily on the sides is a charming idea to soften the black background.

Who said that men mind wearing flowers on their feet? The bright blue background makes the roses luminous and the slippers great fun to wear.

This late Victorian slipper is interesting because of the variety of stitches used: *gros point* for the background and *petit point* and satin stitch for the floral motif.

Slipper Bazaar

To show as much detail as possible of this coat of arms an 18 hole-to-the-inch canvas was used. The design was executed in cotton against a wool ground.

This zig-zag was designed and embroidered as one of a pair by a gentleman for himself. The simplicity of the repeat pattern as well as the colours make it very elegant.

The Prussian Imperial Eagle with its wings spread wide seems to survey majestically the deep black space surrounding it.

The 1830s saw the innovation of a new form of footwear: the embroidered carpet-slipper. Ladies having embroidered their way through the rest of the household with pelmets, footstools, cushions and suchlike, now turned their attention to their loved one's feet.

In 1830, *La Mode* described some carpet-slippers worked in tapestry in a Turkish design, and a pair in Berlin wool which were 'so well calculated for birthday presents and souvenirs'. A poem entitled 'The husband's Complaint' by M. T. Morall in 1852 suggests however, that not all these love tokens were welcome:

> I hate the name of German wool, in all its colour bright;
> Of chairs and stools in fancy work, I hate the very sight;
> The shawls and slippers that I've seen, the ottomans and bags;
> Sooner than wear a stitch on me, I'd walk the streets in rags.

To make carpet-slippers, first one needs a correct foot-template so that the design can be applied and once embroidered, the panels are handed to a shoemaker who then turns them into finished slippers.

Plus ça change, plus c'est la même chose. Slippers are still favourite birthday presents and the sequence for making them has not changed.

The dolphin design above on the front of a slipper is part of the owner's family crest. It looks quite dramatic in gold thread against the trellis background which is dotted at random with the family initial.

17

Country Pursuits

The venerable oak tree is an integral part of the history of England. It is much admired for its numerous qualities and many proverbs cite its virtues. In ornament, its leaves and fruit – the acorn – have been carved and embroidered liberally. The owner of this slipper chose the pattern not only for its symbolism but also for its elegance. What is more, the rich autumnal colours of the leaves against the dark blue ground are evocative of cold winter evenings when one feels like relaxing in a comfortable pair of slippers by the fire.

Never in my wildest dreams did I ever imagine myself embroidering an original Jim Dine. It was his wife who made it possible, by suggesting that I ask Jim to do something special for Peter, my husband. Jimmy immediately agreed to design a pair of slippers, and shortly afterwards I received a call from him saying that he was on his way from his studio with the sketch and canvas. A few minutes later he arrived on his bicycle, and we spent hours selecting the wools: dark shades for the left slipper which represented 'Night' and paler shades for the right one which represented 'Day'.

I was initially nervous about this project but, in hindsight, it was one of the most enjoyable pieces of work that I have ever done. The design was outlined on the canvas with a black permanent marker, and all I had to do was to follow the colour chart that Jim had painted and numbered on tracing paper. I remember that I could not wait to start one colour and then another, and I loved sewing the hearts which are, of course, a major motif in Jim's work.

Jim Dine's Hearts

The slippers were meant to be a surprise birthday gift for Peter, and I was careful to work only when he was away or out of the house. One day however he walked into the room unexpectedly and caught me in the act! He immediately recognized Jim Dine's unmistakable work, and from then on never left me in peace until I finished them!

Cushions

Needlework was much appreciated by Louis XIV and he commissioned an immense number of pieces for Versailles. Gobelins and Beauvais were founded respectively in 1662 and 1664 and produced an abundance of wonderful woven tapestries. At the same time, Colbert, who was Louis XIV's brilliant Finance Minister, had just founded the 'Compagnie des Indes', which began importing Indian calicoes which were extremely influential on needlework design in the seventeenth century.

The flamboyant poppy heads – or *pavots* – with feathered petals, acanthus leaves and coiling tendrils, opposite, are very reminiscent of the Gobelins tapestries. This design was executed in tent stitch with a yellow background which complements the scarlet and pink of the blooms.

The pomegranates and flowers on the other cushion are very stylized and illustrate the great fashion for exotic blooms and fruits that prevailed during the seventeenth century.

Pavots and Pomegranates

The dramatic colour contrasts for this piece were inspired by the woven Italian cut-velvet designs of the late sixteenth and mid-seventeenth centuries. Shaded effects were achieved by cropping and trimming the velvet pile. These were mainly produced in the Genoa region where there was a long-standing tradition of silk-weaving. The shaded effect of the velvet is gloriously reproduced in this cushion design by using different colours of wool. The rich, regal colour combination of gold and scarlet was popular in the sixteenth and seventeenth centuries, not only for court use but for ecclesiastical vestments and altar frontals, while the tightly worked, repeat palmette design with only small areas of ground showing through is characteristic of the period.

Genoese Flame

The cushion on the previous page is based on a seventeenth-century design and has a dense overall pattern with a central strapwork motif from which the highly stylized floral patterns emanate.

From the cushion overleaf one can see that in the seventeenth century in France, needlework had become increasingly rich, with more use of coloured silks and wools and large repeat designs – quatrefoil, fleur-de-lis and geometric patterns which evoke the bejewelled effect of stained glass windows.

Both England and France in the eighteenth century were experiencing a golden age in every possible creative field, including needlework. This enchanting George III tent-stitched panel was worked around 1760. The central design of the overflowing basket of lilies, tulips, primulas and peonies which emblazons the greater part of the panel is contrasted with the delicate trelliswork through which the more humble honeysuckle is entwined. This, together with the ivory ground, serves to lighten what could otherwise be a rather heavy, overpowering composition. (The panel was probably intended originally as a firescreen.) The matching suite of furniture comprising a pair of Chippendale armchairs and a pair of sofas was worked by various members of the Godolphin-Osborne family at Hornby Castle, in Leeds.

There were great similarities between the tent-stitch canvas works of England and France at that time. However, in France there was a preference for ivory as a ground colour, together with a predilection for a more formal style in needlework. Although the honeysuckle trellis panel is an undeniably English interpretation of the subject, the use of a cream background hints at a French influence.

Honeysuckle Trellis

These charming cushions show the versatility of the trellis motif. The most sophisticated cushion of the three is the one photographed on the right. The subtlety of the shading, the finesse of the composition of the trellis, with carnations and roses framed by a row of beads and enclosed by a trailing ribbon with soft bows on each corner,

French Trellis

is simply enchanting. It is so beautifully executed that while it is a joy to study, it is almost impossible to copy. It is embroidered in silk in the basket-weave tent stitch, or *point de St Cyr*, named after the school founded in 1684 by Madame de Maintenon who retired there after the death of her husband King Louis xiv. Girls were sent to this school to learn the art of embroidery and canvas work, as well as for academic study.

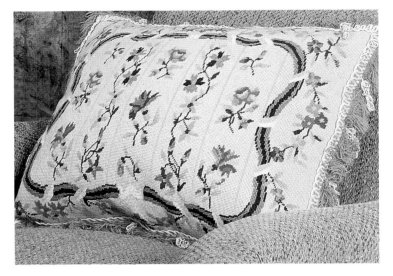

Needlework was a highly respected pastime during the eighteenth century and one which Louis XV himself enjoyed – he even understood the intense feelings that it generated. History records that he quarrelled violently with one of his friends, Madame de Mailly, because she was so absorbed in her needlework that she did not hear him ask her one question, then another and then several more. He became so annoyed with her that he pulled a pair of scissors from his pocket and cut her canvas into pieces. The silence between them lasted for some time and was the endless talk of the salons.

The eighteenth century was the golden-age of ravishing mistresses and they shaped the style and taste of the time. Needlework patterns were bright and delicate and flowers were an endless source of inspiration. The compositions were symmetrical and exquisitely delicate, the bouquet being rather thinner than its seventeenth-century counterpart. They were often framed by a garland of rose sprigs or a ribbon, and stripes intertwined with a floral climber were also popular.

Floral sprays and Garlands

Mrs Godfrey Bradman is a compulsive buyer of needlework designs and equally enjoys the painted or *tramé* pieces. 'When I am in a mood', she explains, 'I sulk with a canvas in my hands, and after a while I feel better.' Although her three daughters tease her a lot about her sulking routine, they all share her hobby which proves that needlework is more often than not an infectious pastime.

Floribunda

Susan likes working on a frame, which is not easily transportable, and like all the other people in this book is working on two projects

simultaneously. She prefers floral designs, mostly French eighteenth-century ones. 'My house is full of cushions now,' adds Susan, 'so perhaps I should think seriously of doing needlework covers for my dining-room chairs!'

Blue Hydrangeas

Susan Bradman hesitated for six months before she summoned enough self-confidence to tackle the blue hydrangea cushion illustrated here. It was the delicate shading of the petals with various coloured wools that she found the most difficult, but the final result was worth all the initial doubts. The design on the cushion is Napoleon III and complements beautifully the cool and immaculate bedroom where it sits next to another cushion –

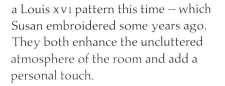

a Louis XVI pattern this time – which Susan embroidered some years ago. They both enhance the uncluttered atmosphere of the room and add a personal touch.

L'amour

This pair of delightfully romantic cushion designs were executed in bright wool and silks. The left-hand one of Cupid and his quiver of arrows and its corresponding partner (where his mission has been accomplished) of two lovers in eighteenth-century dress, were used as central vignettes. The cushions were actually worked in about 1890 to 1900 and they reflect

the nostalgic revival of late eighteenth-century styles which was prevalent in the decorative arts at that time. The yearning for the seeming pastoral romance, elegance and frivolity typified by the court of Marie-Antoinette, is perfectly captured.

Mrs Charles Hambro was for ten years the fashion editor of *The Daily Telegraph* and her excellent eye and wonderful sense of colour are evident throughout her home.

She is a very tidy and neat person which she says inhibits her creativity and, as a result, prevents her from fulfilling her secret ambition of designing her own canvasses. This is our only point of disagreement.

Cherry is fully committed to her hobby and pursues it most vigorously during the shooting-season or on aeroplanes. Like most people portrayed in this book, she works at two or more projects simultaneously: usually one small one which she can travel with, and another, larger piece on a frame. 'But,' Cherry complains, 'each piece of needlework finished means a stronger pair of glasses every year!'

Hambrosia

The design of the cushion shown in close-up overleaf is copied from an old scrap of needlework found in a flea market in Oxfordshire. Typically Victorian in style, Cherry was determined to imitate its intricate design and to capture the original subtlety of colour. It is also the first piece that she has initialled and dated, a practice that she now applies to all her tapestries.

The profusion of different patterns in this bedroom, such as the roses and paisley fabric on the walls, the tartan lampshades, the painted Italian bed and the needlework pictures on the wall, shows that sometimes more is not less. The Arum Lily and Cabbage Roses cushion resting on the bed is typical of the Berlin woolwork designs. The lily is beaded while the rest is in *gros point*. This genre of needlework first appeared in Berlin in the early 1800s when an enterprising German began printing paper patterns. The pre-painted grid enabled one to create a picture without the help of a professional artist, by counting the squares, following the colours and filling the mesh with either a cross or a tent stitch. The new technique made needlework more accessible and through mail order reached a widespread number of people all over the Continent, Great Britain and America. Although some deplored its negative impact on the creative aspect of original canvas-work designs, it did enable those with modest talents and means to afford and enjoy tapestry.

Arum Lily and Cabbage Roses

Paisley and Roses

The pine cone or paisley pattern, as it has come to be known, became popular in the early years of the nineteenth century. It was introduced as borders on Kashmiri stoles and

shawls which were imported. As the craze for these shawls grew, the wool weaving and printing mills in Paisley in Scotland adopted this pattern in its stylized form.

The passion for Paisleys reached its zenith around 1850 and it is interesting to note that this design found expression also in the popular Berlin woolwork. The advent of the rich aniline dyed wools provided the dynamic colour contrasts which are so typical of the shawls from which this design was inspired.

Against the bright new wools of the nineteenth century, black was often preferred as the background colour in deference to Queen Victoria's state of mourning. By the 1850s, beading had become an increasingly popular technique, the finest beads being made in France. As the decade progressed, the Berlin work, of which these are examples, became coarser, the wools more lurid and the designs more improbable and more eccentric, including flowers that were larger than life, romantic scenes and follies.

Folly and Roses

Berlin woolwork became a fad in the nineteenth century. It was taken everywhere: travelling, visiting and even to afternoon teas. At one time, over 14,000 patterns were made available on the market.

When Lady McAlpine took up needlework a few years ago, it was for two major reasons. The first was that her husband, Alistair, had just undergone open-heart surgery and Romilly had to spend long hours in hospital by his bedside. The second was that she had recently given up smoking and needed a therapeutic pastime to distract her. She found needlework both enormously comforting and absorbing and has never looked back.

The projects that Romilly has undertaken are countless and she is always thinking well ahead to the next one. The thought of being left with nothing to do is simply unbearable. She prefers designs where no shading is involved because she finds them more restful to embroider. The cushion pictured here was her very first attempt at needlework and it complements her beautiful Arts and Crafts interior. The design is French, nineteenth-century, when geometric patterns, exotic birds and bouquets of overblown flowers were the fashion in needlework.

Variations
on a Mosaic

From time immemorial, the vine has occupied a unique place in civilization, its grapes and leaves have been endlessly used in wood carvings, sculpture, painting and of course needlework. Noah, according to the Book of Genesis, was the first wine grower; the Egyptians buried their dead with food and wine; the Greeks worshipped the wine God, Dionysius; the Romans adored Bacchus and the streets in Pompeii were lined with bars serving wine. Louis xiv, who loved to be portrayed in classical guise, was even immortalized as an unlikely Bacchus in a sculpture.

This beautiful French eighteenth-century cushion of a grapevine was almost certainly part of a larger panel. The design is embroidered in wool and the highlights and imperial yellow ground in silk. There are five colours in each grape and the subtlety of the shading is simply marvellous. It must have been embroidered either by a professional or by some lady of great talent considering that, in those days, the design was simply outlined on the canvas and not painted because the water-resistant paints we use today had not then been invented.

Grapevine

Beaded Grapes

Berlin Repositories in the nineteenth century sold everything required by the needlewoman, including the much appreciated fine French-made beads which were sold by weight and colour. She was advised to buy the entire quantity of beads she needed in order to avoid the problem of matching sizes and colours if she ran out of them. The

same applies today with the purchase of wools, especially for backgrounds. The very fine needles required to thread through the beads were called straws. Even these were often too wide to fit through the minuscule holes and therefore the thread had to be waxed and then pushed through the bead and canvas.

The Victorians seemed at one point to favour the muted tones of fading autumnal foliage and grisaille beadwork set off against a scarlet ground, as one can see on both these pieces.

Both these designs were inspired by damasks manufactured during the French Empire era and can be executed in two colours only. The effect is different with every colour combination, as one can see here. Not only do the colours create a pleasing effect but also the heavily defined vine leaves contrasting with the more delicate coiling tendrils.

Venetian Grapes and Vine Leaf Trellis

The fact that both designs can be repeated endlessly makes them attractive for use in all sorts of upholstery.

63

This adorable family is living happily in a chalet on top of a Swiss mountain. They are dearly loved by their owner, who commissioned this cushion. The artist was able to capture their expressions by relying on good photographs, and although they seem to be in a loose grouping, there is a very strict social order to the composition. Petunia the donkey is towering above all the dogs but it is Dimitri, the West Highland Terrier, who is in reality the leader of the pack. He dominates completely Zoe the Wolfhound, Rose the Bulldog, Max the Mongrel and Stephanie the Cocker Spaniel.

The rose border, inspired by an eighteenth-century design, is particularly pretty and softens the solemn look on the animals' faces.

Pets, for some, are a way of life and it is hardly surprising that they feature so prominently in needlework, that being one more way to commemorate their friendship and loyalty.

Petunia and her Family

The Duchess of Windsor had no fewer than ten cut-out pugs painted on velvet, standing to attention on a sofa at the foot of her bed. Pugs have been much sculpted and painted and needlework design has also produced many versions of them. Lora, illustrated here, is a cut-out similar to the ones owned by the Duchess of Windsor but in needlework.

The Pekinese dog is inspired by one of the scenes in the Lady and the Unicorn tapestries which are exhibited at the Musée Cluny in Paris. However, instead of attempting to produce an exact replica, this design is composed of a selection of elements that have appealed to the embroiderer, which makes the cushion more personal and charming.

The Labrador cushion was commissioned to commemorate the life of the older, golden one and to celebrate the arrival of the black one to replace it. The festive red ground makes it more joyful and enhances an otherwise plain composition.

Man's
Best Friend

Mathilde
and Rover

Beading is a simple technique: instead of a stitch you place a bead on every square of the canvas. This incredibly fine example was probably worked around 1840 when beads were much finer than those made after 1850. They are minuscule and more commonly found on smaller pieces such as purses and pin-cushions. This piece must have been a labour of love, especially by candle- or gas-light.

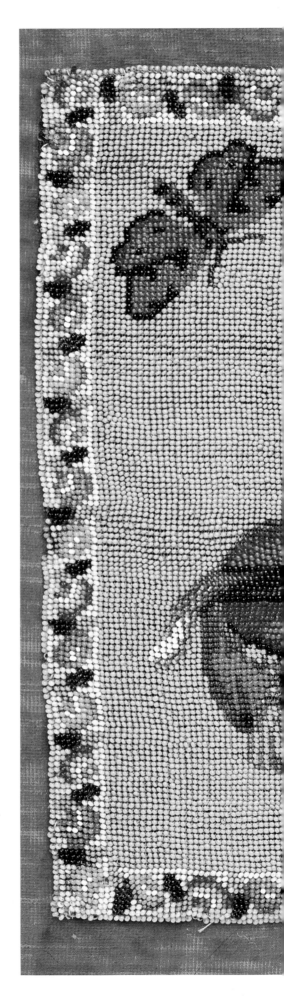

The best way to capture the expression on a dog's face is to embroider the eyes, nose and mouth first, as was done here. Although this is a contemporary portrait of Mathilde, a much loved friend, a sense of nostalgia is created. Her endearing face is framed in an oval medallion suspended from a bow and is reminiscent of Victorian cameos.

In the Edwardian era the famous toy manufacturers, Deans, produced calico sheets on which animals and dolls had been printed. This was a useful and educational exercise for children as they had to cut out the shapes and stitch them together, and were rewarded with an attractive toy of their own making. This tabby cat could be a modern version of the same concept although it would obviously require much more skill and concentration.

The kitten in the hat is probably a mid-nineteenth-century French design. Unlike English needlework, which consisted almost entirely of heavy Berlin wools, this delightful design incorporates a lustrous buttermilk silk *gros point* ground. The central design is delicately and competently worked in *petit point* using fine wools while the whiskers are defined by long stitches in silk. Subjects such as this one continue to delight modern needleworkers just as they did in the 1850s.

71

The fascination for using pets in needlework began with Queen Victoria who passionately loved her own. She embroidered a fire screen panel which is in Osborne House on the Isle of Wight. It features her Highland Terrier, Islay, and her King Charles, Tilco, in conversation with her red Macaw, with Osborne in the distance. Presumably Queen Victoria's pets were very well behaved to have posed for this, just like the adorable kittens looking in awe at their feathery friend on the cushion pictured here.

Parrots and Ducks

In the mid-nineteenth century parrots were a very popular subject for their colourful plumage, while today mallard ducks in flight have become a clichéed evocation of English field sports.

This cushion panel is copied from a Renaissance design and is executed in *gros* and *petit points* using naturally dyed wools. It takes its inspiration from crewelwork designs, seen in the shaded central rock, from which emanate flowering branches, and the strapwork border interspersed with acanthus leaves.

The strong rich colours and colour contrasts, particularly of vivid reds, are typical of the sixteenth century. The finely embroidered bird and the festoon shape of the outer border, make it a perfect example of the great refinement in design and canvas work of that period.

Renaissance Bird

This charming and whimsical design is the exact replica of a photograph in a wildlife book of a tiger resting in the middle of the jungle. Whether on his own, as a pair or even as a trio, the design remains as amusing and as enjoyable to embroider.

Wild animals are great favourites nowadays but tigers, leopards and elephants seem to top the list. This cushion is particularly attractive not only because of the subject but also because of the great care its owner has taken in mounting the piece of needlework as a cushion. A particularly attractive idea is to lift a patterned element from the main design and frame the panel with it; the tiger-skin border, seen here as a detail on the left, enhances the dramatic effect and has been further offset by trimmings and corner tassels.

Resting Tigers

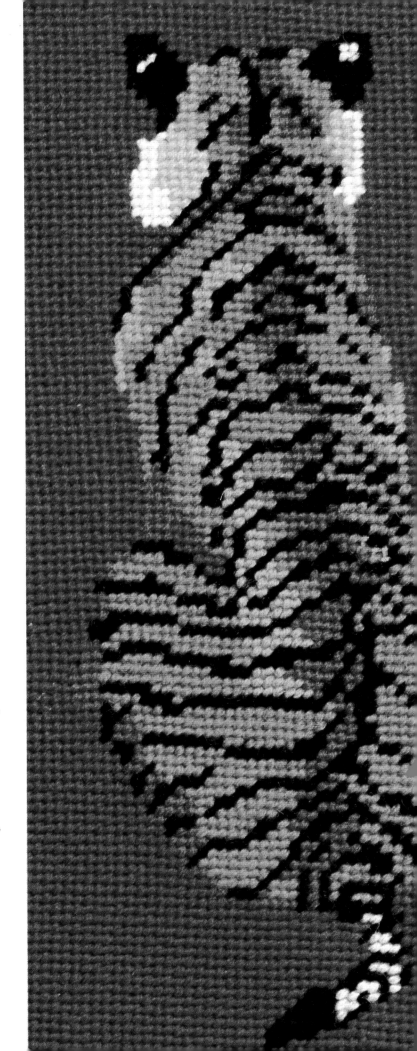

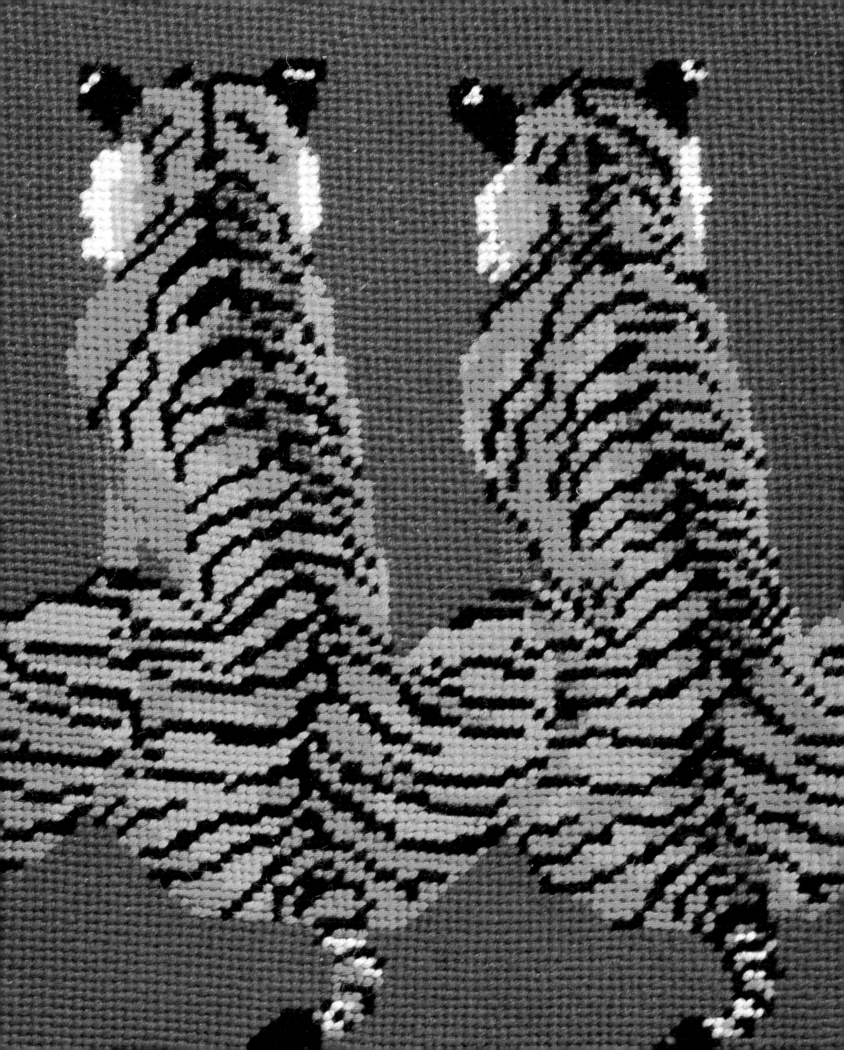

Chairs

Although this chair is very much in the French Regency style, its needlework cover was worked in the spirit of the rococo movement. The name rococo was coined in the eighteenth century and derives from the two French words *rocaille* and *coquillage*: rocks and shells. In their stylized form these shapes are abstracted into scrolls and counter-curves – both major ingredients in this design. Flowers with fronded edges are lavishly spread across the canvas, balanced by coiling tendrils, acanthus scrolls and intertwined leaves.

Rococo

The exciting movement in this composition is dramatically matched by the bold use of colour and set off by the yellow ground echoing the decorative paintwork.

Fruits of
the Earth

The ball and claw chair with its richly carved legs and fretwork back is a fine example of Chippendale's design and workmanship. The French seventeenth-century fruit composition of exotic pomegranates, cherries and figs complements its masculinity, and its strong colours and overall asymmetrical design are typical of the period. The seat was embroidered in a half-cross tent stitch which gives the impression of ribbing.

The exquisite needlework seat cover on the Louis XVI Montgolfière painted chair is almost literally strawberries and cream. It is executed in basket-weave tent stitch, or *point de St Cyr*, with naturally dyed wools, while the diapered ground is embroidered in silk.

By the middle of the eighteenth century, fashion had turned its back on the heavier, bolder shapes and colours of earlier decades in favour of pastel shades and delicate, elongated arching fronds as exemplified by the designs of Robert Adam. The wild strawberries on the back and seat of the Louis XVI medallion chair are another charming variation on the strawberry theme.

'I started needlework during my second pregnancy', says the Countess of Harewood. 'I had to lie in bed for the last three months and a friend gave me my first canvas.' This was an owl which is now proudly framed, 'not for its beauty', explains Lady Harewood, 'but because of its sentimental value!' The Countess has come a long way since that first piece. She is now an expert at needlework and is also a member of the council of the Royal School of Needlework.

For Lady Harewood, there is nothing more restful than stitching her canvas at home at Harewood House while enjoying the splendid view over the terrace, into the park which was landscaped by 'Capability' Brown in the eighteenth century. The canvas on the easel is a chair cover, the second one that she has embroidered. It is a copy of the original chinoiserie design. The armchair, a Chippendale in the French style, is one of four and each cover is of a different design. She chose to do the prettiest rather than the most worn. 'I love shading', confesses Lady Harewood. 'I like mixing two colours of wool in the same needle to create a subtle effect and it is the nearest I can get to painting, which I have little talent for.'

Overleaf, Lady Harewood is photographed in the Adam library which is in the centre of the house. It is one of the rooms open to the public but which the Harewoods like to use during the winter months when the house is closed to visitors. 'It is the nicest and friendliest room in the house', she explains. 'We enjoy using it very much – rooms lined with books are always so welcoming!'

A Countess at her Tapestry Frame

A Harewood Chair

When Thomas Chippendale furnished Harewood House in the mid-eighteenth century he recommended to his clients that French chairs must be covered in either tapestry or needlework. His workrooms often provided patterns for such furniture and it is therefore quite likely that the armchair photographed here was covered in an original Chippendale design. Lady Harewood decided to embroider a new cover when it was no longer possible to restore the old one. The Royal School of Needlework proceeded with the commission by examining the reverse side of the back, seat and arm covers. It is surprising how much one learns about the person who embroidered it by doing this and how fresh the original colours remain. It was probably the first Countess of Harewood who originally covered the chair in about 1770. It was all in silk but the Countess had no sense of economy. She criss-crossed the canvas from one end to the other to avoid stopping and starting if she had to use the same thread. The present Countess embroidered the copy in wool with highlights in polished cottons because the chair is very much used by family and friends.

Fauteuils
à la Reine

Pretty and delicate Mrs Clovis William McAlpin does not shy away from ambitious and often difficult projects. She is a perfectionist with refined taste and great commitment. Her biggest challenge was undertaking two sets of identical chair covers for a pair of Louis XVI gilded armchairs. Although they took a long time to finish, the result is stunning and a source of great pride for Annabella and her husband. Mr McAlpin is a voracious reader while Annabella is an avid

needleworker. 'We talk between a page and a stitch,' she adds 'which is perfect bliss.'

Annabella puts a lot of thought into choosing the right fabrics and trimmings that will be used for making up the cushions she embroiders. 'It makes such a difference when one gives that part of a project more care', she explains.

Directoire Tulips

The Directoire was a turbulent period in French history following the Revolution of 1789 when the old kingdom of the Bourbons had been turned upside down. Symbols associated with the monarchy and their luxurious lifestyle were completely rejected and a sense of social equality set the new standards. As always, design was influenced by this change in mood. Simplicity and gracefulness became fashionable and as a result late eighteenth-century needlework patterns are much plainer than previously seen, but nonetheless a high degree of elegance is maintained.

This Directoire armchair personifies the period. It is altogether a very serene and quiet composition with an almost masculine interpretation of a floral subject, which is refreshingly different on the back cover and seat.

Scattered Roses

This comfortable armchair — a *bergère-crapaud* — has been in the same French provincial family since the 1860s when it was embroidered. The design of scattered roses is very romantic and the repeat pattern makes it dramatically rich against the midnight blue ground.

It is embroidered in wool with silk highlights and, although much used, it is in remarkably good condition.

The elaborate Berlin woolwork upholstery
of this Victorian low chair – also called a
nursing chair – with its dramatic scarlet
ground was worked around 1850. Before
this time, delicate pastel-coloured grounds
or even unworked canvas were popular.
After that, strong almost dazzling colours
were favoured to set off the designs which
tended to be of exotic flowers. The arum
lilies, gloxinias and water-lilies incorporated
in this design are typically mid-Victorian;
the home-grown cabbage rose and flowers
of the field have been discarded in favour of
hothouse beauties grown in conservatories.

On the left an oakleaf and rosebud design is
illustrated, also from the mid-Victorian
period.

Victoriana

Auriculas and Quatrefolia

The small black bentwood child's chair is upholstered with a charming piece of needlework: it is a bunch of auriculas in soft pastel colours against a cream ground with a fan-edge trimming. The chair fits very well in this nursery even though the frame is all black.

The two black *faux*-bamboo chairs are perfectly at home in this richly decorated bedroom. The stylized peony set in a quatrefoil – a symmetrical four-lobed leaf – against a counted-stitch background resembles the medieval stained glass windows so much admired in the nineteenth century. In fact, there was such a fashion for medieval and gothic cathedral motifs at this time that the style became known in France as *Le Style Cathédrale*.

The chair seats are identical in design, the only difference being the reverse colour combination on each ground.

I once came across a photograph of a chair in a decoration magazine and have always remembered it as one of the most beautiful and exciting things I have ever seen in canvas work. It was a French, gilded, Louis XVI chair whose owner had had a Cubist painting by Braque copied and embroidered in shades of grey and taupe. The combination of the Louis XVI style and Cubism struck me as particular stunning. Years later, while antique hunting in Paris, my husband Peter and I came across a very pretty Louis XVI medallion chair which we immediately bought, hoping that we would be able to persuade the celebrated American artist Jim Dine to paint a cover design for it.

We hesitated very much before summoning enough courage to propose this to him, but we should have known better! The result is spectacular but very intimidating because I am not sure that I will be able to do justice to the design with my needle. As usual, Jim took a lot of time and trouble in selecting exactly the right shades of colour in wool, cotton and silk. It is interesting that its composition is very much in the spirit of a Fantin-Latour still-life painting, and in sympathy with the chair's traditional French design. The chair-seat, back and arms are each different, which will make the project even more challenging.

Jim Dine
Flowers

FRONT

Chinoiserie à la Française

At the end of the seventeenth century, the French established commercial bases in Canton, and from this contact a new style arose which became known as Chinoiserie. Charming daily scenes of Chinese life were depicted with great accuracy and yellow, which was the imperial colour of the ruling Ching dynasty, became a favourite ground colour.

Unlike traditional European designs at this time – which favoured large

central motifs, geometric order and symmetry – the Oriental pieces had a flowing asymmetry set against an uncluttered background which was much copied in Europe.

In these exquisite English pieces worked around 1700–10 West meets East. They are in imitation of Oriental lacquer screens and faithfully depict scenes of daily life: Orientals at work and play in traditional Chinese interiors and among exotic gardens surrounded by fretwork. There is no hint of European style except in the use of the tightly worked tent stitch – the Chinese used satin stitch and French knot in their pieces.

Chinoiserie was very popular throughout the eighteenth century and the famous writer Daniel Defoe was heard to complain:

> Queen Mary introduced the custom . . . of furnishing houses with Chinaware . . . piling the China upon the tops of Cabinets, scriptoires, and every chymeny piece . . .

Chinoiserie
à
l'Anglaise

Stools

This extremely complex piece of needlework, with its overall design of spot motifs of birds, beasts and flowers and its dominant central image of the Tree of Life, was inspired by a series of tapestries woven in Tournai in France around 1460, which are now to be found in the Musée Cluny in Paris. The original six tapestries, known as the Lady and the Unicorn tapestries, took as the main subject a richly robed and bejewelled lady, her standards supported by a lion and a unicorn, on a background entirely covered with flowers, among which various animals play.

Tree of Life

At this period, it was popular to cover areas of sky and ground with these motifs, seemingly with no consideration of scale, size or realism, thus lending an added charm and naivety to the pictures.

Elephants are Amanda Ward's obsession. They are everywhere in her home and she has designed many canvases on the elephant theme, including a rug, a party purse, a spectacle case and various cushions, not to mention the most spectacular one, Saleema, which is mounted on a stool. She found the idea of the grisaille elephant in an illustrated children's book, but the floral border was inspired by a pair of large eighteenth-century Aubusson tapestries that hang on the staircase of her home. Amanda says that towards the end of every project, she sits and stares into space, thinking of the next.

Saleema

Small footrests are a charming and refined addition to any interior. The Louis XV footstool, above left, is upholstered with a very pretty design typical of the eighteenth century. It is a floral trellis motif embroidered in wool and using silk for the ground.

The ebonized footrest, below left, is covered with a nineteenth-century Napoleon III pattern, probably copied from a grid published in the *Journal des Demoiselles* which at the time carried a regular pattern feature for its readers. It was in fact the French equivalent to the Berlin woolwork which had swamped Europe at that time and standardized the art of needlework.

Scattered roses and stripes create a particularly charming effect on the *faux*-bamboo stool to the right. Empress Eugénie, wife of Napoleon III, was so infatuated with Marie-Antoinette that she introduced a new style which became known as 'Louis XVI—Impératrice' — a flamboyant pastiche of the original Louis XVI style which was more restrained and delicate.

Pot-Pourri

Swags and Grecian Key Motif

This extremely attractive fender footstool combines both beadwork and Berlin woolwork and the voluptuous cabbage roses are typical of the 1860s. The imaginative combination of the linear Greek Key motif with the swags lightens and enlivens what could otherwise be a rather heavy and stilted design.

The name 'Berlin wool' is commonly used for Victorian canvas works as this is where most of the wool originated. It came from the fleeces of Marino sheep from Saxony which were taken to Gotha to be spun and then to Berlin to be dyed.

The beadwork design of this fine fender stool lends itself perfectly to the shape of this hybrid Louis xv-style piece of furniture. The sharp turquoise colour, complemented by touches of grey and pink, and the palmette shapes of the design are heavily influenced by Islamic art and are particularly reminiscent of glazed tiles.

Palmettes

In the 1860s Orientalism was becoming increasingly fashionable. Painters such as Lord Leighton and Burne-Jones were fascinated by the art and culture of the Near East and the Orient, so much so that the former created in 1865 a tiled 'Arab Hall' in his London house. In the field of needlework, patterns for both Berlin woolwork and beadwork were produced to enable every needleworker to introduce a little of this romantic eastern charm into their homes.

This exquisite beadwork pelmet was worked around 1850, using French beads. It might originally have enhanced a window or mantle but has been put to good use as a striking border to this stool. The row of dragonflies along the top is most unusual and a charming addition to the pattern of arum lilies and exotic blooms.

The rich colours and strong pattern of this clever star-shaped, or rosette, medallion are reminiscent of the Gothic Revival style, as exemplified by the work of A. W. N. Pugin, the famous Victorian architect and designer. It is particularly suitable for a stool cover.

116

Pelmet and Rosette

Rugs

Nothing can compete with the charm of an attic bedroom: here the sloping ceiling, dark wooden beams and charming *toile de Jouy* fabric in a restful blue throughout are irresistible. The striking *gros point* rug fits perfectly in to this scheme. Its design is early seventeenth-century and the formal, almost geometric strapwork trellis is redolent of Tudor blackwork embroidery or even *reticella* – a form of cutwork and whitework embroidered lace. It is believed that such interlaced strapwork was introduced by the Moors travelling to England via Spain and is more commonly seen in English knot gardens of the time.

Blue-and-White Strapwork

This decorative carpet border was most certainly inspired by the Savonnerie woven tapestry carpets made in France in the eighteenth century. The warm golden hues of the wools and silks against a cream background are typical of that style. In the eighteenth century, hardwearing worsted was used for the body of the ground with silks for highlights only. Nowadays, cotton is a perfectly good alternative to silk because it is stronger and more affordable.

Acanthus leaves, coiling stems and foilage, together with the shaded colours on the bloom, combine to recreate a feeling of late rococo work. The application of this elaborate border to a plain piece of carpet transforms it from an everyday utilitarian object to a highly decorative and important feature of the room.

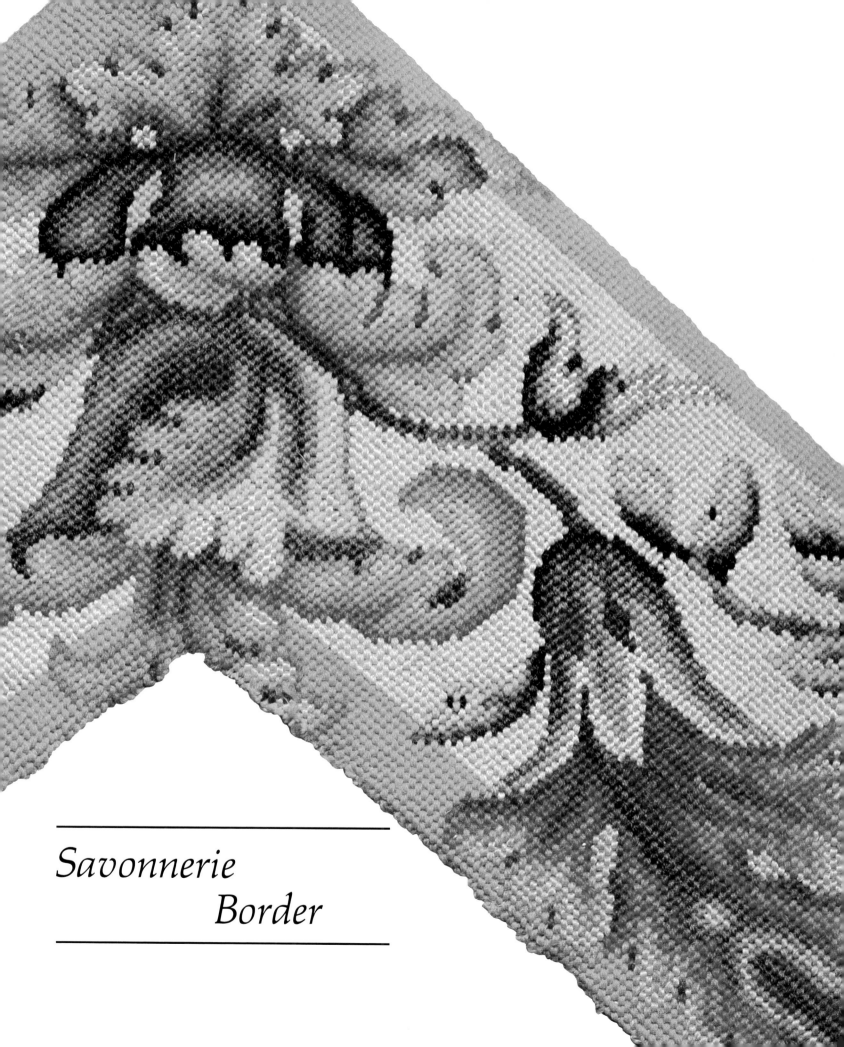

Savonnerie
　　　Border

This basket-weave tent-stitch rug contrasts the delicate feminine repeat pattern of the rose sprigs with the more masculine and exotic grounding of the leopard spots. This unusual design is a French late eighteenth-century piece.

Leopard Spots and Roses

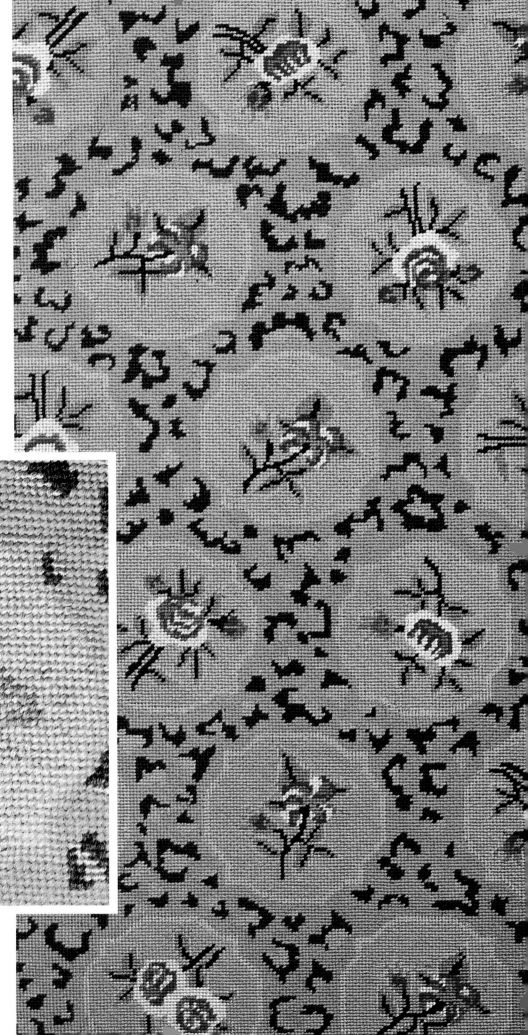

The rose sprigs are very stylized and the leopard spots herald the fashion for animal pelts as upholstery during the forthcoming Napoleonic reign.

During the Directoire and Empire periods in France, needlework design had become formal and quite rigid. Mythological subjects or Empire symbols such as the laurel leaf, the eagle, the bee or simply the initial 'N' for Napoleon became the order of the day. The restoration of the monarchy in 1814 marked a change of taste to a softer and a more comfortable mood. Floral wreaths and bouquets of large flowers became fashionable in needlework and mirrored the new Romantic mood that was captivating nineteenth-century Europe. This needlework rug perfectly illustrates the new spirit. Carnations, cabbage roses and wheat are intermingled with foliage to create a well-balanced cluster in the middle of the design, framed by a simple border to enhance the elaborate centrepiece.

Tapis Romantique

129

Emblems and Novelties

SUB CRUCE

Heraldic canvas work is a statement of status, and it is nice to think that it may have been worked by successive generations of the same family in one form or another over hundreds of years. In the Tudor period heraldic decoration was used to embellish beds, banners, purses, carpets and even painted portraits. However, heraldry for domestic decoration in the form of table carpets, cushions, fire screens or pictures was not common until the late sixteenth century.

Coats of Arms

On the previous page, three offertory bags are illustrated. They were commissioned for the church of St Stephen Walbrook in London, and they display the coats of arms of the Alternate Patrons, The Worshipful Company of Grocers and Magdalene College, Cambridge, and of Keble College, Oxford, of which the Rector is an Honorary Fellow.

The Stanhope Banner

The Honourable Steven Stanhope is a rare bird. He is the only man I approached who has agreed to be photographed in this book as a 'needleman'. It was his wife, Maureen, who taught him how to embroider when they got married twelve years ago. He is now excellent at his hobby and completely relaxed about it. 'Whenever I find myself under pressure', he explains, 'I get lost in my canvas work and the effect is immediately soothing.' He has a sharp connoisseur's eye for good needlework but considers himself totally unartistic.

The idea of embroidering a banner with the Harrington coat of arms was hatched after visiting Glamis Castle, the Queen Mother's hideaway in Scotland. The Stanhopes had seen a banner there, hanging above a bed, and were so impressed by its magnificence that they decided to commission a tapestry design of their own to commemorate the title, which has been in the family since the sixteenth century. It was Maureen alone, however, who worked over 1600 hours to finish this stunning piece of needlework which measures thirty-six inches by fifty-four. It will no doubt become a prized heirloom to future generations of the family.

A DEO ET REGE

Needlework should be both beautiful and functional: it must please the eye but it must also serve a practical purpose. Nowhere is this better illustrated than by the example of the lowly doorstop, which prevents the slamming of a door and thus the fraying of nerves.

Doorstops

Shaped to the size of a brick (a well dried one to prevent the growth of mildew), the range of patterns to cover the doorstop is infinite.

The ribbon and bow design is a witty solution and plays on the parcel-shape of the brick. A particularly attractive idea is to choose different coloured bows for different rooms, depending on your interior decoration. Flowers are also appealing and can be mixed with fruit such as strawberries or cherries to create a more cheerful effect.

The proportions of a Georgian façade, a long barn or a chalet lend themselves perfectly to a house-portrait doorstop.

A case protects you from the pointed end of the scissors and is invaluable to anyone who sews, particularly those who travel frequently or who tend to lose their scissors. They are perfect vehicles for experimenting with new design ideas and even finishing touches, such as piping.

Spectacle and Scissor Cases

These four spectacle cases are particularly appropriate as gifts. Floral motifs are popular but one could equally well select a geometric pattern or even initials or animals – the possibilities are endless and each side need not reflect the other.

With the mid-nineteenth-century madness for tapestry, it was only a question of time before the lady of the house, having exhausted practically every other possibility in the home, turned her attention to both spectacle and scissor cases. Nowadays they are just as popular; they are quick to finish and they make ideal presents.

The striking colour combination of green and turquoise creates an iridescent effect. The colour ways of the design are reversed on the opposite side.

Tea Cosy

Can you think of anything more English than a tea cosy? In the Victorian period, partaking of tea was more than just a question of quenching one's thirst; it was almost a sacred ritual. It was only natural that while the pot was brewing, or after the tea had been poured, it should be cosseted in the finest of tea cosies, and this was a perfect vehicle for showing off one's skills as a needlewoman, especially during the Victorian era, when this example was made.

Although they are used only one night a year, Christmas stockings are very popular. Mothers love making them for their children and sometimes even for their husbands. The variety of subjects is infinite, ranging from fairytale, cartoon or nursery rhyme characters, to more traditional Christmas subjects, and personal designs. Mothers often say they enjoy embroidering them very much because they feel like children with a colouring book. They find not only the subject fun but also the freedom to use the bright colours.

Stockings like these do make Christmas more special, not just because of children who really love them and the treasures they yield, but also because of the nature of needlework. When we were moving house a few years ago, I simply could not find our stockings anywhere. It was just before Christmas so I gave up my frantic search at the last minute and replaced the missing stockings with baskets which I painted hurriedly in bright red. The look on the children's faces on Christmas Eve made me shrink with guilt. The next year, the children demanded to be given their stockings as early as September to keep in their own bedrooms. They wanted to make sure that that terrible episode never happened again.

Christmas Stockings

Name Cushions

Mrs Charles Riachy must have covered miles of canvas with needlepoint, and her immense warmth and enthusiasm are characteristics which are manifested in her work. She never does things by halves, and her home is full of her work in all its variety: a chair in the study, a huge stool in the drawing-room, a rug in her bedroom, slippers for her husband and dozens of beautiful cushions throughout. When Doris decided to give her three daughters a name cushion each for Christmas, she tackled all three canvases at the same time.

The results are charming and children understand how valuable such work is especially when it is dedicated to them.

144

This fine beadwork reticule was made around 1830. Its elongated drawstring shape is typical of early nineteenth-century purses, while the cabbage roses are an intimation of the full-blown Victorian extravagance in design which was to follow. Purses were essential pieces of female equipment in the early part of the nineteeenth century as dresses were so diaphanous that they could not contain bulky pockets, which would have spoiled the slim vertical lines so fashionable then.

The purse on the right is a professional Viennese *petit point*, made between 1900 and 1920. The design is an oriental pastiche, with central pine cones bordered by peacock feather spandrels and Chinese-style clouds.

Embroidered purses, or sweet bags as they were known in Tudor England, were frequently given to Queen Elizabeth I. They were worked by professional embroiderers in the finest silks and silver and gold thread and were popular and important presents in Elizabethan England, especially when they also contained 'angels', as gold coins were known.

The evening purse to the right is of ivory satin. This balloon shape became popular around 1910. The traditional ribbon swag and wreath of roses is typical of the Edwardian period.

Party Purses

147

Counted Stitch
Designs

Choosing tapestry designs to blend in with an existing interior scheme requires a sensitive eye, particularly if the room is already rich in pattern and colour combinations. The repeat pattern of counted-stitch designs is very popular for this reason. It creates a discreet yet striking design that beautifully complements floral schemes. The deep pink rosebuds enclosed in a diamond grid in this Louis XVI design for a fire fender-cover is a stunning example. The armchair cushion is also counted-stitch but of a much bolder design, yet it is equally at home with the floral chintz.

Rosebuds and Diamonds

The fender-cover in this morning room was embroidered by Eve Jackson, a member of the Embroiderers' Guild and a veritable doyenne of the counted stitch. The detail of her work in progress illustrates how an overall pattern is built up by repeating a motif *ad infinitum*. The design is not painted on to the canvas but instead the number of stitches in any colour and direction is recorded by counting, and repeated until the required area is filled. This stitch suits people with a clear, mathematical mind, like Mrs Jackson. According to her, the secret of counted stitch is simply to count and count again. And again. The variety of designs is enormous and makes a pleasant change from floral patterns.

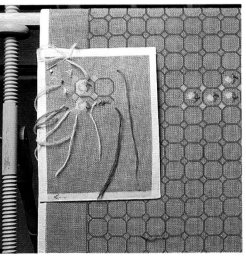

Kaleidoscope

The conservatory reached its apogee in the Victorian period with improved methods of glass manufacture, glass and iron construction, and efficient heating methods. It was only natural therefore that when looking for a design which would blend into a modern conservatory, a mid-Victorian design, reminiscent of encaustic floor tile patterns, so popular in these Victorian conservatories, was chosen.

154

In deciding on a pattern to cover the seat of this late eighteenth-century English Chippendale wheelback armchair, it was important that the design should be simple, unfussy and rather masculine in feel. Opting for a counted-stitch design was the logical solution. The small geometric repeat pattern complemented the clean light lines of the chair without drawing the eye away from its magnificent carving, and it also blended nicely with the decorative style of the library interior. It was important that the covering should be able to cope with the wear and tear of daily use, so the seat was worked with wool.

Spokes and Wheels

STYLE CHART

A comparison of English and French period styles

Dates	England	France
1590–1660	Elizabethan	Late Renaissance and Louis XIII
1660–1700	William & Mary and start of Queen Anne style	Louis XIV
1700–1730	End of Queen Anne and beginning of Palladian style	Regency
1730–1760	Palladian, Chippendale and Georgian	Louis XV
1760–1789	Adam and Neo-classical style	Louis XVI
1789–1804	End of Neo-classical style	Directoire
1804–1815	Regency	Empire
1815–1830	Regency (George IV and William IV)	Restoration
1830–1848	Victorian	Louis-Philippe
1848–1900	High Victorian	Napoleon III
1900–1918	Edwardian	Modern Style

The above dates are a rough guideline to the periods of the styles and do not necessarily coincide with the reigning years of the kings and queens to whom those styles are related.

GLOSSARY

Petit Point or Continental Tent Stitch is when the needle is held diagonally but moves in horizontal and vertical rows creating a thick ridge of yarn on the reverse side of the canvas. The size of the stitch is regulated by the canvas mesh and requires a large quantity of wool.

Gros Point or Point de Croix means cross stitch. The first line is worked with the stitches going from right to left and the second row of stitches go over this line in the same holes of the mesh to form a cross. The needle should be stabbed through the canvas up and down.

Point Droit or **Half-Cross Tent Stitch** looks like lines of back stitch on the reverse side of the canvas. It is economic of thread.

Point de St Cyr or **Basket-Weave Stitch** produces a woven effect on the back of the canvas and is worked on the diagonal starting with one stitch and gradually adding one more on either side and so on.

Bargello or Florentine Stitch is worked in a step arrangement but the length of the stitches can endlessly be varied.

Gobelin Straight Stitch is worked with vertical stitches over two threads of the canvas. On the reverse side each line of stitches faces in the opposite direction to the other like a chevron pattern.

LIST OF SUPPLIERS

Cobb's Needlepoint 217A North Federal Highway, Hallandale, FL 33009, (305) 457-8880

Dunwoody's Needle Accent 5477 Chamblee-Dunwoody Rd., Dunwoody, GA 30338, (404) 393-9322

Joan's Needlecraft Studio 145 East 27th St., New York, NY 10016, (212) 532-7129

The Knotting Chamber 3257 S. E. Hawthorne Blvd., Portland, OR 97214, (503) 232-1043

Needlepoint, Inc. 251 Post St. # 202, San Francisco, CA 94108, (415) 392-1622

Shay Pendray's Needle Arts, Inc. 2211 Monroe St., Dearborn, MI 48124, (313) 278-6266

Sign of the Arrow 9740 Clayton Rd., St. Louis, MO 63124, (314) 994-0606

Thistle Needleworks 63 Hebron Ave., Glastonbury, CT 06033, (203) 633-8503

Wallis Mayers Needlework Inc. 30 East 68th St., New York, NY 10021, (212) 861-5318

Yarn Barn of San Antonio 4300 McCullough, San Antonio, TX 78212, (512) 826-3679

INDEX